T0413724

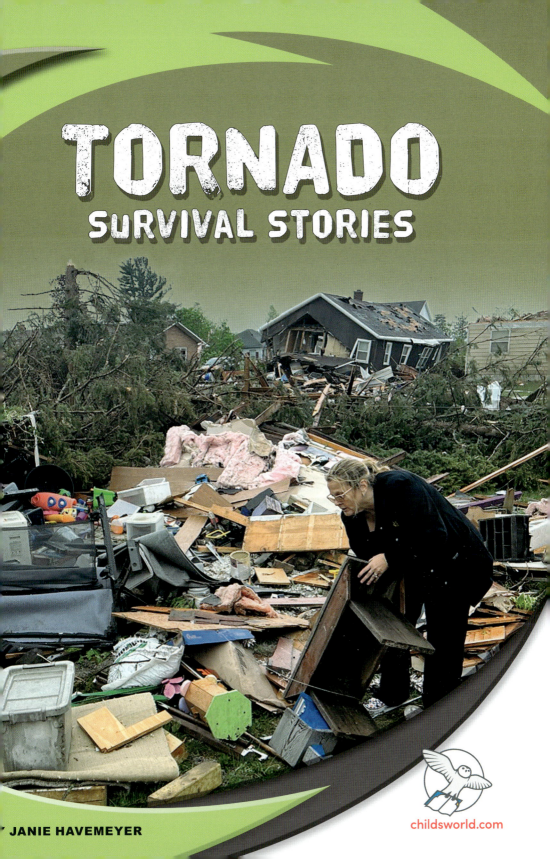

TORNADO
SURVIVAL STORIES

BY JANIE HAVEMEYER

childsworld.com

Published by The Child's World®
800-599-READ • www.childsworld.com

Photography Credits
Photographs ©: John Russell/Detroit News/AP Images, cover, 1; Minerva Studio/Shutterstock Images, 5; Darryl Brooks/Shutterstock Images, 6; Chad Robertson Media/Shutterstock Images, 9; Benjamin Simeneta/Shutterstock Images, 11; Alex Erwin/ Shutterstock Images, 12; Sue Ogrocki/AP Images, 14; Red Line Editorial, 15, 18, 28–29; Ryan C. Hermens/ Lexington Herald-Leader/AP Images, 16; Gerald Herbert/AP Images, 19; Alexey Stiop/Shutterstock Images, 20; Shutterstock Images, 22 (top), 22 (middle), 25 (middle), 25 (bottom); Maike Hildenbrandt/ iStockphoto, 22 (bottom); Emilia Ungur/Shutterstock Images, 23; Monkey Business Images/Shutterstock Images, 24; Satenik Guzhanina/Shutterstock Images, 25 (top); Vash Hunt/AP Images, 26

ISBN Information
9781503854536 (Reinforced Library Binding)
9781503854819 (Portable Document Format)
9781503855199 (Online Multi-user eBook)
9781503855571 (Electronic Publication)

LCCN 2023937263

Printed in the United States of America

CONTENTS

WHAT IS A TORNADO?

A tornado is a powerful, twisting column of air that stretches from a **supercell thunderstorm** to the ground. The United States has around 1,200 tornadoes every year. They can happen at any time, but they develop most often between March and July. Tornadoes have different shapes. Some are very wide while others are thin and ropelike. Tornados suck up **debris** as they move. Flying debris can cause a lot of damage. Most tornadoes are weak and only last for a few minutes. But strong, violent tornadoes can last for more than an hour.

A tornado's strength is measured on the Enhanced Fujita (EF) Scale. The scale estimates a tornado's power by looking at the damage after it hits. The highest rating is an EF-5 tornado with winds above 200 miles per hour (322 kmh). The average speed of a tornado moving across land is 30 miles per hour (48 kmh). When tornadoes hit populated areas, they can cause widespread destruction and take many lives.

FAST FACTS

► An EF-4 tornado hit Cookeville, Tennessee, on March 3, 2020. It had winds of 175 miles per hour (282 kmh).

► On April 12, 2020, an EF-4 tornado hit Moss, Mississippi. Its winds were recorded at 190 miles per hour (306 kmh).

► Mayfield, Kentucky, was struck by an EF-4 tornado on December 10, 2021. It had winds of 190 miles per hour (306 kmh).

► An EF-3 tornado slammed into Salado, Texas, on April 12, 2022. It had wind speeds of 165 miles per hour (266 kmh).

► On January 12, 2023, an EF-2 tornado hit Selma, Alabama. The storm traveled almost 23 miles (37 km).

CHAPTER ONE

SURVIVAL IN A BATHTUB

J ust before 2:00 a.m. on March 3, 2020, Seth Wells was jolted awake. His cell phone buzzed, alerting him to a tornado warning. Wells and his girlfriend, Danielle Theophile, lived in Cookeville, Tennessee. Wells had been through tornado alerts many times, but nothing had ever happened. He got up and looked out a window. Lightning flashed in the sky, but everything else was eerily still. Then Wells heard a sound like a roaring train, and he knew a tornado was approaching.

Wells rushed to wake up Theophile. Their house didn't have a basement to shelter in. So Theophile suggested taking cover in their guest bathroom at the center of the house. They raced there. Wells tried to grab his dog, Mando, but the dog was frightened and ran away.

◄ Outdoor warning sirens often turn on when dangerous events, such as tornadoes, are approaching. They warn people to seek shelter.

By the time Wells and Theophile reached the bathroom's tub, the house had started to shake. Within seconds the house lifted into the air. Wells and Theophile clung to the side of the tub. The house smashed into trees and shattered apart. Wells and Theophile landed 600 feet (183 m) from where they started. The couple had been in the tornado for only 30 seconds. Their house lay in piles of rubble around them.

Wells moved his limbs to see if anything was broken. Everything felt OK. Then he looked over and saw that Theophile was stuck under part of a wall. Wells staggered upright and used the rest of his strength to push the wall off Theophile. They both had cuts and bruises, but they were alive.

Wells looked around at the damage. Trees had been uprooted. Wooden planks from the house were scattered around him. Then he saw bobbing flashlights approaching. He started yelling at the top of his lungs for help. Neighbors helped the couple. They brought Wells and Theophile into what was left of their home, which had been ripped in half by the tornado.

As Wells and Theophile sat on a couch, Wells thought about his parents. "My parents had taught me some of the warning signs, such as dead wind before it hits, and I could hear my mom's voice tell me 'tornadoes sound like trains,'" Wells said.

Tornadoes may completely destroy one ►
building but leave others standing.

TORNADO EF SCALE

The EF Scale ranks tornadoes and breaks down the damage they can cause.

EF Rank	Wind Speeds	Damage Caused
EF-5	200 miles per hour (322 kmh) or more	Well-built homes may be ripped apart and other buildings may have severe damage. Trees are left branchless and their trunks are snapped.
EF-4	166 to 200 miles per hour (267 to 322 kmh)	Well-built homes are torn apart, walls made of stones or bricks may be ripped down, and cars are flung far from where they started.
EF-3	136 to 165 miles per hour (219 to 266 kmh)	Well-built homes will have severe damage, and homes that aren't as sturdy may be carried away. Trees may have some of their bark stripped off.
EF-2	111 to 135 miles per hour (179 to 217 kmh)	Well-built houses may have their roofs torn off, and **mobile homes** will be demolished. Big trees will be uprooted or damaged, and cars may be flung around.
EF-1	86 to 110 miles per hour (138 to 177 kmh)	Houses will have moderate damage such as broken windows or damaged roofs and doors. Mobile homes will have more severe damage and may be tipped over.
EF-0	65 to 85 miles per hour (105 to 137 kmh)	There will be a little damage to a house's siding, roof, and gutters. Tree branches may be broken off, and small trees could be torn down.

▲ Debris from tornadoes can be dangerous. People can get hit
by flying, heavy objects or get buried beneath rubble.

The decision to hide in the bathtub had also helped the couple
survive. The tub had been a sturdy capsule during their
30 seconds in the air.

The tornado made Theophile realize that there was no one
else she wanted to tackle life's challenges with. She turned to
Wells and asked if he would marry her. Wells smiled. "Of course I
will," he said.

CHAPTER TWO

THE SAFE ROOM

It was Sunday, April 12, 2020, and Andrew Phillips and his family were watching a church service online. He decided to flip on his radio and listen to reports on the severe storms pummeling southern Mississippi. Phillips realized a tornado had formed and was heading toward their home in Moss, Mississippi.

He told his wife to grab their young kids and hide in their house's concrete safe room. Phillips stepped outside to see the weather for himself. A funnel cloud had formed in the sky. He raced back inside to join his family in the safe room.

The Phillips family lived in a part of the southern United States that is known for its violent and deadly tornadoes. Phillips knew that having a safe room in his house could save his family if disaster struck. The safe room was specially built to withstand winds up to 250 miles per hour (402 kmh). It was made of concrete blocks. Phillips and his wife used it as a clothes closet. But in case of tornadoes, it would also protect them. It would shield them from snapped trees and flying debris that become wind-borne missiles when a tornado tears up an area.

Less than a minute after Phillips joined his family huddled in the safe room, he heard the tornado approach. Phillips threw his body over his children. He heard a thunderous rumble. The wind roared. There were sounds of ripping and tearing. Phillips felt his ears pop as if he was diving deep underwater. Then he heard a huge boom, like a tree toppling over. He prayed the safe room would protect them like an armored tank in battle.

▲ A safe room like this one saved the lives of Andrew and Amber Phillips and their kids, who were two years old and six months old.

Once the sounds outside died down, the Phillips family crawled out from the safe room. It was as if a bomb had exploded outside. Everything was torn to pieces. Their house was destroyed. The only thing left standing was the safe room.

The severe weather in southern Mississippi that day produced 19 tornadoes. The tornadoes injured almost 100 people and killed 14 others. Eight of the people who died had lived in Moss.

The tornado that hit Moss was rated EF-4. It was 2.25 miles (3.6 km) wide—the widest tornado to ever hit the state. Phillips decided to build another safe room in his next house. No matter what it cost, "it's peace of mind," he said.

STATES WITH THE MOST TORNADOES

On average, some states get more tornadoes each year than others.

CHAPTER THREE

THE CANDLE FACTORY

Tornado sirens cut through the air in Mayfield, Kentucky. It was 9:00 p.m. on December 10, 2021. At the Mayfield Consumer Products factory, more than 100 people were working hard to get products ready for the Christmas holidays.

Flor Almazan was making candles by placing candle wicks in little jars of wax. Isaiah Holt was mixing chemicals in the fragrance department. Marco Sanchez was working as part of a work-release program at the local prison. After the sirens blared, Almazan hurried into a narrow hallway. It had no windows and was the strongest part of the building. The space filled up quickly, forcing everyone to stand elbow to elbow. Almazan prayed she could get home to her daughter, Cristina. Then there was a mighty roar.

The building began to rock, and the lights flickered. The roof peeled away. Then the walls caved in. The next thing Almazan knew, she lay pinned under shattered pieces of the factory. She heard people screaming for help and cell phones ringing. Almazan gasped for air. She could see a gap in the bricks that had buried her, so she twisted her face to suck air from the small crack.

Holt was pinned under rubble, too. Chemicals from the production process burned his back and legs. It was hard to breathe, and his chest ached. He could feel a body at his feet. Holt grabbed his cell phone out of his pocket and pressed the video button. He wanted to show his family and friends what had happened and tell them he loved them. The hours ticked by.

Eventually, Holt's cell phone battery died. He closed his eyes and prayed for a miracle.

Sanchez lay in a pile of rubble as well. He had a broken leg and ribs, but fear gave him the strength to dig himself free. As Sanchez sat on top of the rubble, he thought he had died and was on his way to heaven. Then he heard crying and a voice calling, "Help me! I'm trapped." Sanchez began to dig until he reached a woman. "My feet hurt," she cried. Sanchez saw she had lost her shoes. He handed over his own pair and helped her to safety.

THE TORNADO'S PATH

The tornado on December 10, 2021, traveled 165.7 miles (267 km) in three hours. At its largest, the tornado was 1.3 miles (2 km) wide. Its winds reached a high of 190 miles per hour (306 kmh).

▲ The Mayfield community came together
to help clean up after the tornado.

Then he went back to digging. "I knew I was needed," he said.
"There was more out there."

Eight people at the factory died. Sanchez saved four people by
himself. Almazan spent six hours trapped under rubble before she
was rescued. "What happened is very difficult to forget," she said.
Holt stayed buried for four hours. "I just remember thinking keep
wiggling my toes to keep the blood flowing," he said. The tornado
was the deadliest in Kentucky history. It killed at least 80 people.

CHAPTER FOUR

MIRACLE IN SALADO

A tornado swept through Bell County in central Texas on April 12, 2022. The Rios family heard the tornado warnings. Vanessa Rios was tending to her baby, Ezra, and six-year-old daughter, Miriam, in their mobile home near Salado. Mobile homes are not safe places to shelter in when the weather is severe.

They are not secured to the ground like a permanent house is secured by concrete. Joel and Vanessa Rios made the quick decision to escape to a more secure area. As Joel drove his family down the dirt road, baseball-sized **hail** made it difficult to see. He decided it would be safer to turn back.

The family huddled together in their mobile home. The **twister** now had 165-mile-per-hour (266 kmh) winds as it sped toward Salado. Vanessa heard the tornado's loud winds as it approached. Their home began to shake. Vanessa clutched Ezra to her chest. The walls began to crack and shatter. Debris flew everywhere. Vanessa grabbed her daughter by the hair as the fierce winds pulled Miriam away. Then Vanessa lost **consciousness**.

Blake Miller was driving by after the tornado passed though Salado. When he heard yelling, he stopped his car to investigate. Miller took a quick scan of the area. Toys and shattered bits of a mobile home lay all around. Appliances had been torn into pieces. He found Joel trapped under tree limbs. Joel pointed to a nearby tree. Miriam was hanging there, upside down, unconscious but alive. Then Miller saw Vanessa, who was badly injured. Only Ezra was still missing. Miller heard whimpering coming from inside a tangle of tree limbs. He began to dig into the pile of branches.

WHERE TO GO DURING A TORNADO

Tornadoes can happen anywhere and at any time. People should know where to take shelter during a tornado warning.

IF people are in a house with a basement,

THEN they should go to the basement and find an area that doesn't have windows. They should hide under something strong, such as a heavy table, or lay underneath a mattress.

IF people are in a house that doesn't have a basement,

THEN they should get to the lowest floor in the house. They should go to a small room in the center of the house, such as a closet or bathroom. People can also shelter in a hallway without windows, or underneath stairs. They should cover themselves with blankets or a mattress.

IF people are in an apartment,

THEN they should get to the building's lowest level. This might be the first floor, or it could be a parking garage underground. They should shelter in the center of the room and stay away from windows.

IF people are in a mobile home,

THEN they should leave. They should seek out a community tornado shelter or permanent building. If that's not possible, people should go outside and lie down on the ground. They should stay away from cars and trees. They should protect their heads.

▲ A tornado's powerful winds can suck up anything in its path.

He found Ezra, who was alive and not badly hurt. The branches had formed a safety dome around Ezra's little body. Each family member had been thrown in different directions by the tornado.

Thirty minutes later, rescue workers arrived. The Rios family was taken to the hospital. As they healed, their community raised money to help them buy a new home. The four members of the Rios family were among 23 people who were badly injured during the Salado tornado.

CHAPTER FIVE

PRESCHOOL HEROES

Sharon Reid was the director of Crosspoint Christian Church's preschool in Selma, Alabama. On the morning of January 12, 2023, she answered a ringing telephone. A parent was calling to tell her that a tornado had touched down and was heading toward Selma. Reid sprang into action.

◀ Teachers tell students what to do if a
tornado warning happens during school.

She was responsible for 70 children. Reid ordered all the teachers

and their students to shelter in the building's four bathrooms.

Reid hustled students into a bathroom. She told them that

things might feel scary. "I will get you through this," she promised.

TORNADO SAFETY TIPS

There are things people can do before, during, and after a tornado
to stay safe.

BEFORE

- People should find safe spots in their homes or places they visit often.
  That way, people know exactly where to go during a tornado warning.
- People can make an emergency kit. It can include things such as water,
  food, and a radio.

DURING

- A tornado watch is when an approaching storm might make a tornado.
  During a tornado watch, people should pay attention to the news and the
  weather. Signs of a storm that may lead to a tornado include a dark-green
  sky, hail, and a funnel cloud.
- A tornado warning is when a tornado is very likely to form or has formed.
  People should find shelter as quickly as possible.

AFTER

- If people are trapped after a tornado, they should call 911. They should make
  noise so people can find them.
- People shouldn't go near power lines that have fallen. They could
  get electrocuted.
- People shouldn't enter damaged buildings.
- People should contact loved ones and check on neighbors.

▲ **A section of the roof of the preschool building at Crosspoint Christian Church caved in during the tornado.**

She told everyone to lie on the floor and close their eyes, as if they were taking a nap. As the tornado got closer, it sounded like the school was sitting under a waterfall. Then the lights flickered off. Some children began to cry. "God is here with us," said Reid to calm the children.

In another bathroom, teacher Shana Lathan tried to shelter her students with her body. "It's OK. I got you," she cried. The walls of the building began to tremble and rip apart. Debris flew around. Amanda McCloud took care of babies at the daycare. She held a seven-week-old baby close to her chest as the roof collapsed around her.

After the wind died down, Reid opened a bathroom door and saw dark clouds above. The ceiling was gone, and the school walls had been shredded into rubble. She also smelled a gas leak. The gas could start a fire or trigger an explosion. Everyone needed to get out of the ruined building as soon as possible. Teachers and children escaped to a nearby field as the rain poured down on them. "I'll never be the same," said McCloud. The experience had left her in shock. But she and the other teachers had saved the lives of all 70 children. The next Sunday, the church pastor David Nichols honored the preschool workers as heroes. "There is no doubt about it," he said. "If they wouldn't have acted swiftly . . . like they did, we might be having a whole different story right now."

THINK ABOUT IT

► What would you do if there was a tornado warning in your area? Where would you go to stay safe?
► Make a list of the best and worst things to do during a tornado. Explain why.
► What are some ways to help people who have lost everything to a tornado?

TORNADO MAP

MINNESOTA

SOUTH DAKOTA

IOWA

NEBRASKA

COLORADO

KANSAS

MISSOURI

OKLAHOMA

NEW MEXICO

ARKANSAS

LOUISIANA

TEXAS

Salado, Texas (2022)

MEXICO

GULF OF MEXICO

WISCONSIN

MICHIGAN

NEW YORK

NEW JERSEY

PENNSYLVANIA

DELAWARE

OHIO

ILLINOIS INDIANA

WEST VIRGINIA

MARYLAND

Mayfield, Kentucky (2021)

KENTUCKY

VIRGINIA

NORTH CAROLINA

TENNESSEE

Cookeville, Tennessee (2020)

SOUTH CAROLINA

MISSISSIPPI

ALABAMA

GEORGIA

Selma, Alabama (2023)

ATLANTIC OCEAN

Moss, Mississippi (2020)

FLORIDA

N
W E
S

GLOSSARY

consciousness (KAHN-shuhs-nuhs): Consciousness means being aware and awake. Head injuries can cause people to lose consciousness.

debris (duh-BREE): Pieces of things that have been destroyed or broken down are called debris. Debris from the tornado covered the town.

hail (HAYL): Hail is solid balls of ice. The storm produced a lot of hail.

mobile homes (MOH-buhl HOMES): Mobile homes are moveable houses. People should avoid being in mobile homes during tornadoes.

production (pruh-DUK-shun): Production is the act of making something. Candles were made on the production line at the factory.

rubble (RUHB-uhl): Rubble is broken bits and pieces of buildings that have fallen down or been destroyed. The tornado turned the town into rubble.

supercell thunderstorm (SOO-per-sel THUN-der-storm): A supercell thunderstorm is a type of thunderstorm that can produce severe weather. A supercell thunderstorm can cause tornadoes.

twister (TWIS-tur): A twister is another name for a tornado. The twister hit the town.

SELECTED BIBLIOGRAPHY

"About Tornadoes," *National Weather Service*, n.d., weather.gov. Accessed 7 Apr. 2023.

Hogeback, Jonathan. "How Do Tornadoes Form?" *Encyclopedia Britannica*, n.d., britannica.com. Accessed 7 Apr. 2023.

"Tornado Basics," *NSSL*, n.d., nssl.noaa.gov. Accessed 7 Apr. 2023.

FIND OUT MORE

BOOKS

Burns, Kylie. *Tornado Readiness*. New York, NY: Crabtree Publishing, 2020.

Crane, Cody. *All about Tornadoes*. New York, NY: Children's Press, 2021.

Tarshis, Lauren. *Tornado Terror*. New York, NY: Scholastic, 2017.

WEBSITES

Visit our website for links about tornadoes:
childsworld.com/links

Note to Parents, Caregivers, Teachers, and Librarians: We routinely verify our Web links to make sure they are safe and active sites. So encourage your readers to check them out!

INDEX